Correspondence Course

Sears Philosophy
makes life livable and lovable.
"The Books Without an If"
teach how

CORRESPONDENCE COURSE
The Psychology of Use
OR
The Extravagance of Economy

by

F. W. SEARS, M.P.
AUTHOR OF

"Concentration and Will-Power," "The Psychology of Abundance,"
"How to Attract Success," "How to Give Treatments,"
"How to Conquer Fear," "Everyday Experiences,"
"Sears Psychology Lessons," etc.

CENTRE PUBLISHING CO.
NEW YORK CITY

Copyright, 1921, F. W. Sears, M P. All rights reserved

HG7931
.S4
copy 2

Ⓒ CI A627675

NOV 10 1921

FOREWORD

The purpose of this Course of Study is not to teach students either to spend or save money, but to teach how to develop such a *consciousness and thought habit* as will enable one to *use* his money so he will attract a constantly increasing abundance of supply to him.

Life on every plane of consciousness is purely a question of relationships; nothing is absolute except Universal Law, and no form is ever perfect except for its kind.

There are a number of men in the United States whose annual incomes are more than twenty millions of dollars.

There are also more men here whose incomes are less than two thousand dollars annually than there are whose incomes exceed that amount.

Money does not turn from the one class into the coffers of the other by accident, chance or luck, but as the result of the *use* each one makes of universal laws.

That those in both these classes use these universal laws unknowingly does not prevent the universal laws from working.

The earth has been revolving in its orbit around the Sun ever since it was created, although the most enlightened men a few centuries ago taught that the Sun revolved around the earth and tortured those who disagreed with them. They are still attempting to do the same thing to-day.

FOREWORD

These Lessons are designed to teach the student what the universal law is that directs this flow of money away from some persons and towards others;

Also how to use this universal law knowingly, constructively and harmoniously, and so be able to direct a constantly increasing flow towards such user.

The underlying principles taught in these Lessons are not new; they have been known to man for ages, but the use taught of universal laws is new.

It is so different and at such complete variance with all former teachings of every science, philosophy and religion with which the world is familiar that the ordinary student is likely to stand aghast with amazement when he first hears them.

There are others who will at once recognize the truth of everything taught herein for their own soul has lived them in consciousness and knows they are true.

The real student always starts to learn his lesson with an open and receptive mind. He knows that unless he is ready to receive what the teacher has to give out, he will make but little progress.

When he finds a statement he is not yet ready to accept as a greater interpretation of truth than he already knows, he does not reject it but begins to study and analyze it more closely.

In order to study these Lessons constructively, one should relax in both mind and body and become receptive to their vibrations.

The strained, tense, forceful condition in which many earnest seekers after knowledge, wisdom and understanding, pursue their quest, should be avoided.

No attempt should be made to memorize the text. One might be able to repeat every word in these Lessons and their answers and still not know the first thing taught in them.

In such a case he would have the *form*, the outer clothing, but would not have the inner meaning or *consciousness*.

The Lessons should be read often, *absorbed* and assimilated.

Not a day should be allowed to pass without reference to them. This aids in keeping their teaching fresh in our memory and we unconsciously absorb and assimilate the *consciousness* back of them.

In this way will the student get into and relate with the finer, more vibrant and harmonious currents where he will obtain a better understanding of the

Author's interpretation and subtle teaching.

The universal law of *use* by an intelligent, constructive and harmonious *consciousness*, is the keynote to these Lessons.

The subtleness of this law and its action can be best understood by those who go deeper than the surface.

The vital importance of this is self-evident to the thinker and analyst.

A *consciousness and thought habit* of harmony by which this subtle universal law of use may be knowingly and constructively applied so one may "eat his cake and have it too," figuratively speaking, is not grown in a day by those who have spent years and incarnations in growing the opposite kind of a *consciousness and thought habit*.

But it can be grown and these Lessons teach how to do it.

Such a *consciousness and thought habit* is the result of persistent study and application, and can be grown by any earnest student who will persist.

Such a *consciousness and thought habit* can be grown by any student in less than half the time it has taken him to grow the kind of a one he now has, and it is *worth the price any one may have to pay in time, effort and study.*

The Author *knows* the truth of this for he does not teach any universal law until he has first tested and proven its truth for himself.

His work then becomes that of a teacher; to teach these universal laws and their application to those who want to learn; he has no desire to reach others nor "convert" any one.

Your work is to prove as much or as little of these teachings as you may desire.

THE AUTHOR.

SPECIAL INSTRUCTIONS TO STUDENTS

When one loves or enjoys doing a thing he gets more out of it than is otherwise the case.

This is because he does it under the Law of Harmony and so both his action and its reaction on him are harmonious and constructive.

The student should therefore study these Lessons with the *feeling* it is his *blessed privilege* to do so. The stronger this *feeling* is within him the more will he get out of the Lessons and the better and deeper will be his understanding of them.

He should remember it has taken years

for him to grow his *consciousness and thought habit of economy,* and while it is possible for him to learn how to change that consciousness in a few hours, yet the *process of effecting the change* usually takes longer than learning how to make it.

The process of *making the change* in anything is purely a matter of use and growth, after one learns how to make it.

How long it will take any one to effect the change in his *consciousness and thought habit,* which these Lessons teach, will be determined solely by the *use* he makes of the knowledge contained in them, and the growth in his *consciousness* resulting from such use.

The amount of time to be given to the study of these Lessons is a matter for each student to determine for himself, but it is wise to give them some time each day.

When their study is taken up one should relax, let go, get as easy and comfortable as he can, then quietly and calmly read over the Lesson or such part of it as he may wish. One should do this as best he can whether he is riding in the subway or in the seclusion of his own home.

One should never attempt to memorize the Lesson. It should be read over carefully and as much of it absorbed as possible, that is, the student should not "work at it," nor attempt to *force, make or compel* himself to understand or remember.

When the student is ready to answer the questions at the end of each Lesson he should take a separate piece of paper, *write his own name and address at the top*, also the following: *"Answers to Questions of Lesson One* (or whatever the number of the Lesson may be) *The Extravagance of Economy."*

It is *not* necessary to write the questions; simply answer them in their numerical order, placing the number only of such question before the answer.

By being careful to follow the instructions in the two preceding paragraphs you will greatly aid in the review of your answers.

The student should remember he is writing these answers for his own benefit, not for ours and that the more he uses his own language in giving his answers (rather than the language used in the text) the more will he show his own understanding of the Lesson.

We would suggest the student write his answers just as though he was explaining the matter to some one who knew nothing about it, but to whom he wished to give as clear and lucid an explanation as he was capable of giving.

When sending in answers for review students may ask any question about the Lesson they desire.

When answers to all three Lessons have been received by us we will mail you a copy of the printed answers without further expense.

These are contained in a book similar to this one comprising about the same number of printed pages. It is a most valuable adjunct to these Lessons.

CENTRE PUBLISHING CO.,

108 AND 110 W. 34TH ST.,

NEW YORK.

Copyright, 1921.   F. W. Sears, M.P.   All Rights Reserved

THE PSYCHOLOGY OF USE
OR
The Extravagance of Economy

by F. W. SEARS, M.P.

Lesson One

Immediately after the announcement of the armistice in the great world war, November, 1918, the call went out for the people of the United States to *economize* so we might pay off the immense debt our country had incurred.

All the other Nations of the world also called upon their people to *economize,* either for the same reason or some other which seemed equally important to them.

Economy; economy; economy; was the cry heard everywhere.

From the administration at Washington to the humble housewife bending over her wash tub;

From the great financiers of Wall Street to the "bolsheviki" orators haranguing the crowd;

From sky-line billboards, merchant's windows, newspaper editorial and advertising columns, has the cry for *economy* been blazoned forth to an ignorant, impressionable and unsuspecting public.

Economy sales of hats, shoes, clothing, gowns, food, and everything else one could think of, have faced us no matter which way we turned.

So insistent have these calls for *economy* been, one would almost be inclined to think that all the money in the world had been destroyed and there was little or no hope of ever being able to get any more.

Conversation with even casual acquaintances seemed impossible without the question of *economy* being brought up in some way.

While in conversation with a well to do business man one day he commented on having his last year's straw hat cleaned up so he could wear it and *economize* in his expenditures.

Let me say right here that it matters not how many old hats, old suits of clothes, old gowns, old shoes, or old anything else we may have repaired and wear, as long as we do so with the thought, the feeling, the *consciousness,* of their being of *use* to us.

It is the thought, the feeling, the *consciousness,* of doing these things for the purpose of *economizing* which is destructive.

It is not the thing we are doing which is destructive, but it is the *consciousness* with which we do it that determines whether its effect is constructive or destructive.

This truth is fundamental in the *Sears Philosophy,* and proves itself whenever we are ready to prove it.

Why the thought, the feeling, the *consciousness,* makes this difference will be more explicitly unfolded to the student as he progresses in the study of these Lessons.

For some time now has the entire world been concentrating on the thought, the idea, the image, the vision, of *economy* and practicing it as best it knows how, and what is the result?

Every Nation in the world *feels* poor

and poverty-stricken, no matter what its financial condition may be.

Shortly after the United States declared war against Germany in April, 1917, our Government, through Secretary Houston, sent out a long and earnest plea for all of our people to *economize* in every possible way so we might have ample means with which to carry on the war.

The response was so quick, earnest and whole-hearted, the effect so sudden and complete, that it was quickly brought home to our politicians, financiers and business men generally that the life blood of the Nation was being sapped at its fountain head by the *economy* of the people.

None of these "great" men had learned the great universal law of *use* (which we see expressed everywhere around us when we look with eyes that see), constructive and *harmonious use,* and that the more we *use* anything under the Law of Harmony the more of it do we have to use; while the less we use of it, or when we use it under the Law of Force, the less we have of it to use.

The Washington administration was soon calling for help and urging the people to at least buy what they really needed in order that business might be continued along more normal lines.

Such reversal of form by the Government was practically telling the people it did not know what it was talking about before and did not mean all it had said.

The damage had been done, however, and not until the people began to see evidences of the extravagant war expenditures of the Government did they cease pinching down in their expenditures, and *economizing*.

While the practice of *economy* ceased almost entirely for the time being, yet the *consciousness* of it remained dormant with the people.

Man seldom learns his lesson from one experience, but usually has to have many of them before he even realizes what the lesson is that he has to learn.

The history of 1920 shows that the experiences of 1917 in the practice of *economy* were again repeated, but without the accompanying inspiration to the masses of the extravagant and prodigal was expenditures by the Government.

The business world experienced a period of stagnation and adjustment which needed but little encouragement to become a panic. Nearly every one we met was curtailing his expenses in order to *economize*, like the man with the straw hat.

Banks curtailed their loans in order that they might be prepared for anything which might happen.

Liberty bonds touched new low levels.

Stocks and bonds of undoubted value were selling at prices way below that justified by both their intrinsic and earning value.

Interest rates increased beyond the legal rates allowed in many states in the frantic endeavor to draw capital to the various industries.

And still the cry went out for yet greater *economy*.

Why do the great financiers, the monied interests of the world, endorse and encourage this cry for *economy,* but refuse to practice it?

Do they understand the universal law of *use* and so know that the less the masses *use* their money the more will they need to *economize* and the longer will they remain slaves in their *consciousness* and so be the easier to exploit?

Should the practice of *economy* in the *use* of money be a wise provision and in full accord with the highest, best and greatest use of Energy under universal law, then *economy* is a wise practice in its application to *all things* and *not* simply in its application to the *use* of money.

One of the very first things our country did after declaring war was to call out all of our young men in order to train them for the arduous duties the work of a soldier entails.

The army and navy officers did not *economize* in their work of developing the muscular and physical strength and the mental power of our boys, but went carefully and systematically at work to bring it out and develop it to the uttermost.

Man has learned that through the gradual, systematic and harmonious development of the muscles of his physical body he can increase his strength and power of endurance (that is, his ability to use Energy through his physical body) to an almost unlimited degree.

He has also learned that by *economizing* in the use of his muscles, or by using them inharmoniously and destructively, he impairs their usefulness, decreases his physical strength and power of endurance, and when this is persisted in for any length of time he becomes physically unfit and an easy prey to disease.

We can, therefore, readily see and understand that *economy is not* a universal law, but is a law which man, in his ignorance, has made for himself.

When we look with eyes that see we cannot help but read Nature's story everywhere which is that abundance, extravagance even to the extent of profligacy, is the universal law.

That the more we *use* of anything under the Law of Harmony the more of it do we have to *use;* while the less we *use* of it, *economize* in our *use* of it, or use it under the Law of Force, the less do we have of it to *use*.

Let us apply this truth to the *use* of

money from a National viewpoint and analyze the result.

Prior to the breaking out of the great World War in 1914, Great Britain was always a creditor Nation.

She became a creditor Nation by reason of the savings of her people as the result of their practicing *economy*.

In other words she became a creditor Nation under the Law of Force by reason of her people straining, striving, scrimping, saving, denying themselves, *economizing,* in their expenditures in order to have something for a "rainy day."

What was the result?

The great World War came along and took away, under the Law of Force, all of her great savings so accumulated, and changed her from a creditor Nation to a debtor one.

Before the World War the United States was always a debtor Nation, that is, it sent more money out of the country each year than it received from other Nations.

As a Nation the United States has always expended its money lavishly, extravagantly, profligately, and yet in the face of this fact and the further fact that she is the youngest of all the great Nations of the world, she is also the richest of them all.

During the war she cancelled practically all of her foreign indebtedness, and from being a debtor Nation at the beginning of the war she became a creditor Nation before the close of the war.

Had it not been for her *consciousness of the abundance of the supply of everything and her oneness with it,* that no matter how much she spent there was always "plenty more" where that came from, she never would and never could have accomplished this result, to say nothing of financing her own war expenditures of twenty-five billions of dollars and the loaning to the allies of ten billions of dollars in addition.

There always will be "plenty more" for her as long as she retains that kind of a *consciousness and thought habit* and works under the Law of Harmony.

The same thing is true of the individual.

When we eliminate the fear habit from our consciousness, whether it be the fear of a lack of money, health, love, strength, courage, social position, business success, political power, or what not;

When we cease to *use* our fear faculties and allow them to atrophy from disuse, using those of courage and harmony instead, we will begin the gradual development of great strength and power through the constructive use of our imagination.

We will continue to grow in strength and power under these conditions until the day will come when nothing will be impossible for us to accomplish.

Having acquired this consciousness under the Law of Harmony there will never be any desire to *use* our great power for any purpose other than that which will be for one's highest, best and greatest good.

Policy will have ceased to be a controlling factor in such a life, while *principle and character* will stand out strong, powerful and unconquerable.

Let us go back a moment and study the effect of Secretary Houston's message of *economy*, made to our people at the outbreak of the war.

This message so completely filled the imagination of our people with the thought and idea of *economy* that they stopped buying even some of the necessities of life, and at once business began to feel the full effects everywhere of this universal stoppage of trade.

The people were deeply interested in carrying on the war to a quick and successful conclusion and were ready to do everything the Government officials thought necessary towards accomplishing this end.

It was this fact that made them respond so quickly and thoroughly to the message of *economy*.

The stoppage of all kinds of business was so quick, strong, powerful and complete, that the Government had to start other propaganda and urge the people to begin buying again to at least the extent of what they actually needed and for which they could pay.

The Government discovered that to shut off the *use* of money through stopping its expenditure by *economizing* was like shutting off the flow of blood in the human body.

The practice of *economy* in the latter case would cause the death of one very soon, but it is no more deadly to the body than is the shutting off of the life blood of the Nation deadly to the Nation.

THE EXTRAVAGANCE OF ECONOMY

The continued free and uninterrupted circulation of money is as much of a necessity to the life of a civilized Nation as is the free and uninterrupted circulation of blood to the life of the individual.

Interfere in any way with the blood's circulation and the individual's life is endangered.

Interfere in any way with the money circulation of a civilized Nation of to-day and its commercial life is endangered.

And yet everywhere in financial, business and political circles, all of which ought to know better, was heard the cry for *economy* and the censure of extravagance.

Extravagance of what? Material things?

Suppose we should destroy everything man has ever created and which is in the world to-day, we could replace them all in a comparatively short time.

But destroy the *consciousness, the feeling,* the knowledge that we have the ability to do this; destroy our *consciousness of the abundance of the supply, and our oneness with it,* that is, our ability to create, and there would be no hope for us anywhere.

Those who have censured extravagance and preached *economy* are the most destructively extravagant of all for they would ignorantly destroy the *consciousness and thought habit of abundance* (in which all material things are first created) in their ignorant *use* of their power.

The greatest and most destructive extravagance man can possibly commit is to grow a *consciousness and thought habit of economy;* this far transcends any material waste or extravagance he can otherwise express.

A *consciousness and thought habit of economy* shuts man away from the universal source of supply, curtails the production of material things—which are the symbols of wealth—and limits his relationship with all material and spiritual things.

Extravagance in the *use* of material things only destroys the material product *after it is created,* while in no way limiting the power to create or lessening the production, but tends rather to increase the latter.

A *consciousness of economy* at first destroys the incentive to create and, when persisted in, will destroy the power and ability to create.

A *consciousness of economy* is business and financial suicide by strangulation.

No greater and more complete, yet subtle and insidiously destructive power can come into the life of the individual or Nation than the development of a *consciousness of economy.*

It is far more dangerous and destructive than is T.N.T., the most powerful explosive known, for it is more subtle and far reaching in its action; its greater danger lies in its being less liable to be recognized or understood as being dangerous and destructive.

No more sure and certain prophecy of the decline to abject poverty of individual or Nation can be found than is the development of a *consciousness and thought habit of economy.*

I know this is heresy of the greatest

kind; that all our former teachings and preconceived ideas are against this kind of philosophy.

So are all of the teachings of the *Sears Philosophy* heretical to our old beliefs.

That is why it is the *Sears Philosophy,* and why the *Sears Philosophy,* is different from every other science, philosophy and religion with which the world is familiar.

Questions for Lesson One

1. What is the most important thing to you which this Lesson teaches?
2. What kind of a *consciousness and thought habit* has the world been unconsciously developing?
3. How may we *use* our old clothes constructively?
4. What truth is taught herein that is fundamental to the *Sears Philosophy?*
5. What is the effect of the world concentrating on *economy?*
6. What was the effect of our Government's call on the people to *economize* when the U. S. entered the great World War in 1917?
7. What was the effect again in 1920?
8. Is the practice of *economy* a constructive or destructive principle, and why?
9. Is the practice of *economy* a universal law or a man-made law, and why?
10. What is the universal law that Nature teaches?
11. How did Great Britain become a creditor Nation?

24 THE EXTRAVAGANCE OF ECONOMY

12. How did the United States become a creditor Nation?
13. Which character of consciousness is the more constructive, and why?
14. Why will there always be " plenty more "?
15. What is one of the destructive habits necessary to eliminate, and why?
16. What is the difference between " policy " and " principle"?
17. Is it good *economy* to stop the flow of blood in one's veins? Why?
18. Why did the Government change its *economy* message of 1917?
19. What is the destructive feature in the practice of *economy*?
20. Why is a *consciousness and thought habit of economy* more destructive than any material waste or extravagance?

THE PSYCHOLOGY OF USE

OR

The Extravagance of Economy

by F. W. Sears, M.P.

Lesson Two

The *Sears Philosophy* is based on an unlimited fundamental principle: — the *manipulation of universal Energy,* the power that creates all form and gives life to it.

All other teachings, scientific, philosophical and religious, are based upon a limited fundamental: — the *manipulation of form* after it has been created.

Methods, which are the manner, system, creed, dogma, rules, regulations, technique, by which all form is manipulated, are *the all important thing* with all scientific, philosophical and religious teachings.

The *consciousness and thought habit* with which all *methods are used* is *the all important thing* in the *Sears Philosophy* teaching.

This is why we teach those who want to learn, to receive and *use* the *Sears Philosophy* to whatever extent they are able to do so, accepting only as much of it as becomes a truth to them, for it is only that much one can *use* constructively.

We can *prove* the truth of whatever we really want to prove.

When we are satisfied to *prove* only a limited interpretation of life then it is worse than useless for anyone to attempt to make, force or compel us to *prove* a larger interpretation.

Ex-President Wilson once said: "War is worth the cost can the Nation be taught to save."

This was the biggest truth he knew at that time.

Is it the biggest truth you know, or want to know?

Is it the biggest vision possible for anyone to obtain?

When we examine the history of Nations we find that the more freely their wealth has been circulated the more prosperous have they been.

Never in the history of the world have the masses had so much wealth, and never has the world generally prospered so much as during the last half century, barring the period of the World War.

The prosperity of Nations began to decline only as wealth became centralized in the hands of the few and its free circulation was curtailed.

This also holds true in the case of the individual.

The United States is the most prosperous Nation in the world's history.

Its people, individually, are the most prosperous of any Nation in the world's history.

Its people are the most intelligent and enlightened, taken as a whole, of any Nation in the world's history.

Its people have always been the most extravagant and wasteful of any Nation in the world's history.

They have never saved their wealth by denying themselves what they wanted, as have the people of other Nations.

Their savings, as a people, have been their surplus over and above what they wanted to expend for their comfort, education, pleasure and upliftment, instead of being made at the expense of these things.

They have always spent their money with a prodigality which caused the people of other Nations to gasp in astonishment and believe we were all millionaires.

It is not what man either spends or retains which counts, but it is the *consciousness* with which he does either one.

As the result of our Government's call for the people to *economize,* their imagination became filled with the fear that unless they scrimped and saved down to the very last crust the war might be lost.

Probably no one went hungry, naked or shelterless in order to effect a greater saving. In fact the "saving" was undoubtedly made up from what had heretofore been wasted rather than from any real savings made because of self-denial.

Such "savings" were, therefore, really a surplus which had never been used before, rather than the effect of any real *economy*.

Had the "saving" been made with the *consciousness* of its being a surplus over and above what we needed or could constructively *use* ourselves it would have been alright, for the image such a *consciousness* stamps on the imagination is one of an *abundance and our oneness with it.*

But when such "saving" is made with the *consciousness* of its being necessary to *economize* then it is most destructive for it stamps an image of lack on the imagination and creates a *consciousness of our separation from the abundance of the supply.*

The objective effect of filling the imagination of the people with the thought of *economizing* did not begin to wear off until the extravagant expenditures of the Government began to show forth in its conduct of the war.

Under the stimulus of the Government large buildings were erected almost overnight. Cities doubled their population in a few weeks time. Entire new towns sprang up with all modern improvements in a few months.

All kinds of labor, both skilled and unskilled, was in great demand, receiving as much for a day's pay in many cases as it had received for a week or more before.

Women were used in all kinds of work, receiving as much in their weekly pay envelope as they had earned in a month or more before.

With all these conditions existing it is no wonder that hundreds of men became millionaires in a few months time.

The huge war expenditures of our Government and the readiness with which billions of dollars were raised to pay the bills soon *filled* the imagination of the people with the image of an abundance and gave them a most opulent vision of the immensity of the supply, coupled with one of extravagance and profligacy.

Business began to pick up again all over the country; prices commenced to soar; profiteers started to make their plans for cornering the supply of necessities, with the result that by the close of the war all kinds of labor had doubled and tripled its wage, shortened its hours of work, and was living better than a king did a hundred years ago; while the luxuries at the command of the wealthy were beyond the wildest dreams of even a generation ago and made the stories of the "Arabian Nights" seem common-place and ordinary.

The new image of opulence and the vision of the abundance of the supply of everything which was unconsciously held before the people of the United States by the immense war expenditures and the supplies gathered for war purposes; the immense sums of money obtained from the people through taxation and war loans, gave them such an inspiration of abundance and lifted them so high up in the opulent currents that there would have been no stopping of their business success, trade expansion, and the gathering in of the wealth of the world, had they remained in and related to these currents of opulence and abundance.

But this was not possible with the *consciousness and thought habit of inharmony* which prevailed among them and laid back of all their words and actions, and the *consciousness* of the Law of Force which had been used by both capital and labor in obtaining their temporary prosperity.

Shortly after the armistice was signed Government officials again began to send out warnings for the people to begin to *economize* so the immense war debt could be taken care of and the Nations of Europe aided in their work of reconstruction.

The so-called labor class was not yet ready to give up its image of opulence and abundance and return to its old economical ways of living.

The abundance of the supply in which the people had reveled was like a glimpse of heaven and they were loth to give it up.

They had never been taught how to acquire a *consciousness and thought habit* of the abundance of the supply and their *oneness with it under the Law of Harmony.*

They only knew the Law of Force and its use and so they took the only means, used the only methods, adopted the only systems with which they were familiar, in order to retain their condition of abundance.

This was the use of force, either physical or mental, by which they could make or compel others to do their bidding. The result was that strikes, shut-downs and lock-outs became the order of the day.

No line of business and no community of people anywhere in the country were free from the effects of this condition.

Strikes to force increased pay and shorter hours are simply one of the methods the Universal Law uses to bring man back to a limited environment when he has used force, either physical or mental, to take him beyond the kind of an environment his *consciousness and thought habits* have grown for him.

When man succeeds in obtaining improved conditions and increased pay as the result of his forcing, making or compelling it to come to him through striking, profiteering, sweating, bribing, or in any other forceful way, no matter how legitimate it may be considered under the law of the land, he always uses such improved conditions and wealth so obtained, in an inharmonious and destructive way which reacts upon him in due process of time.

We need only to study Germany's wonderful history of industrial growth since 1870 and prior to the war to fully appreciate this truth.

There never is any real injustice in the world; it only seems such to our human consciousness because we do not look deeply enough into the universal law of cause and effect or action and reaction.

Man is always entitled to everything he gets, no matter how he gets it, for he can never get anything, good or bad, which he has not built for himself in some way through the *character* of the thoughts he has allowed to persist in his thought world.

When he gets what he does not want there is no one upon whom he can justly place the responsibility but himself.

That he does his work ignorantly, unknowingly and unconsciously makes no difference to the Universal Law for it is always at work, but it does make the biggest kind of a difference in the effects which man receives.

The universal law under which we obtain a thing, whether it be the Law of Force or the Law of Harmony, determines our *use* of that thing be it money, health, love, courage, strength, friends, or anything else.

That man has obtained almost everything he has ever had through using the Law of Force does not prevent him from obtaining still more for a while, but it does affect his *use* of it and his ability to retain it.

The time comes when he finds his ability to obtain what he wants grows less and less the longer and more powerfully he uses the Law of Force.

The people of the United States as a whole have had less of this *consciousness and thought habit* of force than have those of other Nations.

This is one reason why their souls have been born into physical bodies which had their birth in this country, or else why they have emigrated here after they were born.

It has been possible for one to relate with and produce the materialized abundance here in the United States much easier than in any other country. The result has been to create a *consciousness* among its people of there always being "plenty more where that came from."

It has been with this kind of a *consciousness* its people have always spent their money, and so there always has been "plenty more" for them as a Nation.

So extravagant and prodigal (unconsciously so perhaps) are we in the expenditure of our national wealth that we pay out over a billion dollars yearly to foreigners for the carrying of our exports to foreign countries instead of having our own shipping with which to do this work and so retain that vast amount of wealth in our own country besides giving us an ample merchant marine in case of any emergency.

The history of the United States and

its people is all against the practice of *economy*. It verifies and upholds the teaching of the *Sears Philosophy* in this respect.

Great wealth in the banking and commercial worlds has only been possible through the free and lavish expenditure of money.

Vast sums have been made in business through the most extravagant expenditure of money in advertising some simple thing and so creating a Nation wide demand for it.

This does not mean that *all* money prodigally, lavishly or extravagantly expended will bring abundant returns or is constructively expended.

We can always do everything in two ways, constructively or destructively;

under the Law of Harmony or the Law of Force.

The *consciousness* with which we do things; the *consciousness* with which we expend or use our money, curtail our expenses, or "save" our money, determines whether the effect will be constructive or destructive.

This is a wonderful truth which cannot be brought to your attention too often, nor made too strong, nor emphasized too much.

This does not mean, either, that man having already grown a *consciousness of economy* should at once begin to *express extravagance before he has even began to grow a consciousness of abundance and his harmonious oneness with it.*

That would be almost as destructive as

to continue to grow a *consciousness of economy.*

It does mean we should first *begin to grow a consciousness* which will enable us to spend what money we do *use* with a *consciousness* of freedom from all fear of lack or the *need to ever economize* at any time.

Each day we should *express* as much of this new *consciousness* in our expenditures as we can without fear or the possibility of regretting our action.

Questions for Lesson Two

1. What is the most important thing to you which this Lesson teaches?
2. Upon what fundamental principle is the *Sears Philosophy* based?
3. What is the basic principle of all other teachings?
4. What is *the all-important thing* with such teachings?
5. What is *the all-important thing* in the *Sears Philosophy?*
6. Is the principle of "saving" in itself a constructive one, and why?
7. Why has the United States been the most prosperous of Nations?
8. What is *the* important thing in spending or "saving" money, and why?
9. When saving is the result of a surplus what is the effect?
10. When saving is the result of *economizing* what is the effect?
11. What was the effect on our people of our Government's extravagant war expenditures?

12. Why did not prosperity for the people continue uninterrupted?
13. What universal law was used in creating their prosperity, and why was it sure to fail ultimately?
14. When man obtains improved conditions beyond that which his *consciousness* has grown for him under the Law of Harmony, what is the result?
15. What determines our *use* of anything we obtain?
16. Why is there no real injustice in the world?
17. What is one of the causes for souls being born in the United States?
18. Why have the people of the United States always had " plenty more " with which to meet all demands made on them as a Nation?
19. Does the history of the United States and its people favor the practice of economy?
20. What should first be done before *expressing* an extravagant *consciousness*, and why?

Questions for Lesson Two

1. What is the most important thing to you which this Lesson teaches?
2. Upon what fundamental principle is the *Sears Philosophy* based?
3. What is the basic principle of all other teachings?
4. What is *the all-important thing* with such teachings?
5. What is *the all-important thing* in the *Sears Philosophy?*
6. Is the principle of "saving" in itself a constructive one, and why?
7. Why has the United States been the most prosperous of Nations?
8. What is *the* important thing in spending or "saving" money, and why?
9. When saving is the result of a surplus what is the effect?
10. When saving is the result of *economizing* what is the effect?
11. What was the effect on our people of our Government's extravagant war expenditures?

12. Why did not prosperity for the people continue uninterrupted?
13. What universal law was used in creating their prosperity, and why was it sure to fail ultimately?
14. When man obtains improved conditions beyond that which his *consciousness* has grown for him under the Law of Harmony, what is the result?
15. What determines our *use* of anything we obtain?
16. Why is there no real injustice in the world?
17. What is one of the causes for souls being born in the United States?
18. Why have the people of the United States always had "plenty more" with which to meet all demands made on them as a Nation?
19. Does the history of the United States and its people favor the practice of economy?
20. What should first be done before *expressing* an extravagant *consciousness*, and why?

Copyright, 1921   F. W. Sears, M P.   All rights reserved.

THE PSYCHOLOGY OF USE

OR

The Extravagance of Economy

by F. W. SEARS, M.P.

Lesson Three

The objective world teaches that Nature is a prodigal, lavish, extravagant producer and spendthrift.

There is no evidence anywhere of Nature ever saving, scrimping or *economizing* in anything.

Everywhere does Nature teach and *use* the abundance and unlimited supply of everything.

Man alone has a *consciousness* of there being any limitation of the supply.

Man alone has a *consciousness* of his

separation from the abundance of the supply.

Man alone has a *consciousness* of limitation and separation which *seems* to make the practice of *economy* necessary.

Man has never suffered from lack because of any limitation or *economy* practiced by Nature.

Man relates with lack (even while he is in the midst of an abundance of whatever he wants) because his *consciousness and thought habits* are too inharmonious to relate him with the abundance.

When man begins to *economize in the use* of anything he then begins to lose his power to *use* it; also his ability to relate with and acquire it.

One of my students wanted to arise earlier than usual, so I instructed him to charge his astral mind with the hour he wished to arise when he went to bed the night before.

He awakened promptly at the hour designated, but decided not to arise and went to sleep again.

Since then he has attempted to awake earlier than usual on several different occasions, but failed to do so and asked the reason why.

It was simply because he failed to *use* his power and so has lost the *use* of it in that direction for the time being.

We can always *regain the use* of any of our power or faculties, but it is more difficult to do so when we have played with them, or *used* them destructively under the Law of Force.

Let man cease to *use* his hands and feet for a few years and they would atrophy from disuse.

The effect of our failure to use any of our faculties is not usually noticed so quickly as in the above case, but such effect always comes in due time.

Nature, or God—the great Universal Law—always relieves us of everything we do not *use,* or which we may *use* destructively. The process is frequently so slow we do not realize it, but it goes on just the same.

This is the way we get rid of anger, hate, worry, fear, anxiety, poverty and lack of all kinds; *we cease to use them; cease to live in the consciousness of our oneness with them;* they then begin to cease to exist for us in just the degree *we cease to use them.*

To *economize* in our use of money, that is, to spend money with the *consciousness* that it is necessary to *economize,* is to create a *consciousness* which not only sees and believes in lack, but which also sees our separation from even what little money our consciousness still believes there is.

When this is persisted in the ultimate effect can only be to relate us with poverty and lack. This is one reason why children are born into an environment of poverty and lack of all kinds.

The creation of a *consciousness of economy* in the use of money not only results in shutting us away from money, but it extends to all other things in due time, for this is a universal law and is applicable to all things; not just money alone.

This is why "the poor ye have always with you." They have a *consciousness and thought habit* of lack and their separation from the abundance of the supply of everything, and so can only relate with lack as long as they retain such a *consciousness.*

We want to remember that man is dualistic in his form, that is, he is both material and spiritual; human and divine.

The human part of man possesses the physical and mental states of consciousness.

The divine part of man possesses the soul and spiritual states of consciousness.

Primitive man, not having developed the mental faculties, lived in his physical consciousness which was inspired by the wonderful dreams and visions of his soul consciousness.

The result was he lived in a literal Garden of Eden and its Paradise of luxury, with an abundance of everything at his command.

create a *consciousness* which not only sees and believes in lack, but which also sees our separation from even what little money our consciousness still believes there is.

When this is persisted in the ultimate effect can only be to relate us with poverty and lack. This is one reason why children are born into an environment of poverty and lack of all kinds.

The creation of a *consciousness of economy* in the use of money not only results in shutting us away from money, but it extends to all other things in due time, for this is a universal law and is applicable to all things; not just money alone.

This is why "the poor ye have always with you." They have a *consciousness and thought habit* of lack and their separation from the abundance of the supply of everything, and so can only relate with lack as long as they retain such a *consciousness*.

We want to remember that man is dualistic in his form, that is, he is both material and spiritual; human and divine.

The human part of man possesses the physical and mental states of consciousness.

The divine part of man possesses the soul and spiritual states of consciousness.

Primitive man, not having developed the mental faculties, lived in his physical consciousness which was inspired by the wonderful dreams and visions of his soul consciousness.

The result was he lived in a literal Garden of Eden and its Paradise of luxury, with an abundance of everything at his command.

All he had to do was to "help himself" to whatever he wanted. There was no personal ownership. Everything was furnished him without work, effort, strain, striving, worry or anxiety.

Life was one long glad song of joy and happiness as he had nothing to do but to "eat, drink and be merry."

This condition apparently palled on him and he became lazy, indifferent and insensible to the finer consciousness of his soul vision.

He allowed the harmonious union between his physical and soul consciousness to atrophy from disuse by reason thereof, and so did human man gradually become *separated in his consciousness* from divine man.

It has been from this faint recollection of the former union with the divine man within us that human man in all ages has created his personal God and made such God separate and distinct from himself.

We want to bear in mind that this separation has only occurred in man's *consciousness;* not between the human and divine forms themselves. They remain connected as long as the physical body lives, and because of this fact it is always possible to reunite them in their *consciousness* as well as in their forms.

This separation in *consciousness* was the natural effect of the causes which produced it. It was simply the effect of universal law which is unchangeable, immutable, irrevocable.

While universal law is unchangeable, immutable, irrevocable, our *use* of it is changeable at any time we so desire and because of this fact man can, through his own work upon himself, *use* this same universal law to grow back the *consciousness* of union he has so ignorantly and unknowingly lost.

Progression, evolution, involution, unfoldment, development, the finer form working through the coarser and the coarser being used and refined by the finer, this is the law of life everywhere on all planes of consciousness.

Life is activity, motion, action, *use*. No standing still anywhere.

As human man began to lose the *consciousness* of his union with his soul consciousness he felt the need of some faculty, greater than his physical consciousness, to guide and direct him in the material world and with which to communicate with his fellow-man.

This was the beginning of the growth

and development of his mental consciousness.

The mental consciousness was first formed from the emanations, the essence, the finer atmosphere, the perfume, of the physical consciousness.

As man's mental power grew and developed strength and power he came to believe that the power which controlled people and things was that exercised by his mentality (but this was only partly true) and so he used every effort to cultivate, refine and make it still stronger and more powerful.

The real controlling power in the *use* of Energy on every plane of consciousness is *thought;* not mental power.

Mental power is only the *limited use of thought by the human mind,* just as physical power is only the limited use of thought by the physical cell consciousness.

Soul power is the more *unlimited use of thought by the soul mind;* while *spiritual power* is the still greater, finer, more subtle and powerful *use of thought by the spiritual mind* incarnate in man.

Human man's *use* of thought by the physical and mental consciousness relates him with the limited universal currents where only the lesser ideals, visions, expressions and supply exist.

Divine man's *use* of thought by the soul and spiritual consciousness relates him with the unlimited universal currents where the larger and more unlimited ideals, visions, expressions and supply are to be found.

Human man, through his physical and mental states of consciousness, only contacts the material things of the objective world, that is, the slower vibrating and more dense forms which his physical senses can cognize.

Human man never contacts the unlimited source of supply from which came the material that produced these slower vibrating forms. He only *knows* of them through the divine man within him.

The materialized supply is always limited no matter how abundant it may seem to be.

The unmaterialized supply of everything, that is, the universal substance from which all form is made, is unlimited.

The more we use of it under the Law of Harmony with which to create form of all kinds the more there is of it for us to use.

Divine man, through his soul and

spiritual consciousness, contacts the unlimited source of supply—the unlimited universal substance—from which all materialized form is created.

Human man, contacting or relating with only the material supply, always attempts to protect himself against some possible shortage in the material supply which he fears may exist at some future time.

This he does by accumulating a surplus of the material supply beyond what he either needs or can use for the time being, as did some of the Israelites in their travels through the wilderness in the gathering of the daily supply of manna.

Human man's *consciousness* of the necessity for such accumulation is the basis for his idea of *economy*.

Human man, being limited in his vision

to that with which he can contact by his physical senses, is always dominated by the visible supply of a thing and his relationship to it.

This is why human man sees lack and the need of protecting himself against it by *economizing* in his *use* of the visible supply.

The practice of *economy* makes for repression, inactivity, non-use, and so shuts one away from the supply.

The human mind can only understand its union with or separation from that which is materialized—never the *source* from which it came.

In seeing its separation from the materialized supply, which causes it to *economize,* the human mind fails to see or understand that the more it *economizes,* represses itself from using, the more it continues to separate itself in its *consciousness* (where union or separation must and does first occur) from the universal supply, and the more will it have to continue to *economize* as long as it continues to grow its *consciousness of economy*.

Several years ago a man came to me saying his income had been so reduced that he could not afford to retain his present home and so he would have to get a less expensive place.

I told him he could take a cheaper place and then when his income was still further reduced later on he could take a still cheaper one and keep on doing this until he found himself out in the street.

Or, he could change his *consciousness and thought habits,* increase his income and remain in the home where he was or move into a still better one as he might choose.

This man decided to take the latter attitude with the result that his income was materially increased in a few months and continued to increase with each succeeding year ever since then.

When man lives in the larger and more unlimited vision his soul and spiritual consciousness give to him he relates with the currents from which the few kernels of corn planted in the ground draw the material for stalk, stem, leaves, and ripened corn at harvest time.

Man then sees this unlimited supply and relates with its source the same as does the intelligence in the kernels of corn, and so relates with it in his consciousness the same as does the corn.

Man's *soul consciousness,* using

thought with which to manipulate Energy by finer methods than is possible with either his physical or mental consciousness, relates with the material abundance as did Moses, Elijah and Jesus of old.

We can establish this relationship and get what we want under either one of two universal laws: The Law of Force or the Law of Harmony.

Forms, things, conditions may be created and relationships established under either one of these two laws.

Every effect is always preceded by the causes which produced it, and every action is always followed by its corresponding reaction. This is again universal law, unchangeable, immutable, irrevocable.

The universal laws always work in exactly the same way. When we *know* this we only have to begin to change our use of them in order to begin to change their effect on us.

Changes in *habits of thought* and the consciousness created thereby, are not made in a day, nor by making an affirmation a few times.

A consciousness of abundance and our harmonious oneness with it can only be grown when we have begun to plant the harmonious thought seeds and continue our cultivation of them.

A *consciousness of economy* is a characteristic of the human consciousness which has been handed down to the human race for hundreds of generations, and so it has become a strong race *thought habit* which is not going to be changed by the wave of some magic wand.

But each life can *begin to change it now.*

We can begin now to grow a *consciousness and thought habit of harmony and our oneness with the universal abundance of the supply* which, as it grows and increases from our continued use, will lift us out of the limited currents into which our *economy consciousness* has kept us and bring us into relationship with the finer and more unlimited currents from which we may draw a supply so unlimited as to be past the wildest dreams of the most avaricious human mind.

We will draw our supply from the same unlimited and inexhaustible source as do the corn, wheat, trees, flowers, the infant in our arms, and all other forms of material life, until like man they learn to practice *economy*.

A *consciousness of economy* is man's greatest extravagance for it invariably relates him with poverty and lack in due process of time.

A consciousness of abundance and our oneness with it under the Law of Harmony is man's greatest asset and is an uncancellable insurance policy against poverty, lack and all other limitations.

We can all grow such a *consciousness and thought habit.*

Questions for Lesson Three

1. What is the most important thing to you which this Lesson teaches?
2. What lesson does the objective world teach about Nature *economizing?*
3. Why does man relate with lack when there is an abundance of everything all around him?
4. What is the effect of man's *economizing* in the use of anything?
5. What is the result when we fail to use our power along any line?
6. Can we regain the use of our power, or of any of our faculties, when we have once lost it?
7. How do we get rid of anger, hate, worry, fear, anxiety, poverty and lack of all kinds?
8. When we *economize* in the use of money what is the ultimate effect?
9. Why is it that " the poor ye have always with you"?
10. Is man monistic or dualistic, and why?
11. What states of consciousness does human man express? Also divine man?
12. What was the effect on primitive man of living in his Garden of Eden?

LESSON THREE

13. Where has the separation of human man from divine man occurred?
14. What is the real controlling power in the *use* of Energy?
15. What is mental power, or mental force?
16. What is soul power?
17. With what currents does human man's *use* of thought relate him?
18. With what currents does divine man's *use* of thought relate him?
19. Why does human man see lack and the need for *economy?*
20. What is the effect of human man living in the visions of his soul consciousness?

Sears Philosophy
makes life livable and lovable.
"The Books Without an If"
teach how

ANSWERS TO QUESTIONS
CORRESPONDENCE COURSE

The Psychology of Use
OR
The Extravagance of Economy

LESSONS

by

F. W. Sears, M.P.

CENTRE PUBLISHING CO.
NEW YORK CITY

Copyright, 1921, F. W. Sears, M.P. All rights reserved.

PREFACE

It has been deemed advisable by the Author in this case to depart from his usual custom in his other Correspondence Courses of not preparing or publishing a standard set of answers to the questions at the end of his Lessons.

He has, therefore, prepared answers to all questions asked in this Course of Study and presents them herewith in connection with the Lessons.

The student should understand that the world is filled with people who possess great knowledge, but who lack wisdom and understanding simply because they have failed to *use* their knowledge.

The learning of the answers to the questions in this Course of Study will enable the student to obtain the knowledge they contain, but unless he is persistent in the *use* of such knowledge he will not gain the wisdom and understanding which he can otherwise acquire through its *use*.

Continued and persistent *use* of the knowledge taught in these Lessons will enable the student to develop the *consciousness and thought habit* by which he can relate with a constantly increasing abundance of anything he may desire, for the universal law of harmonious *use* is applicable to all things and is not confined simply to money and muscle.

While the Author has no desire to proselytize, nor convert anyone, through argument or otherwise, he is always ready to answer any question and give any further explanation of any point in these

Lessons upon which the earnest student may wish additional information.

There is no charge for this service as it is included in the regular price of the Course of Study.

Questions outside of and not germane to the Lessons cannot be considered by the Author except by special arrangement.

THE AUTHOR.

Answers to Questions

THE PSYCHOLOGY OF USE

OR

The Extravagance of Economy

Lesson One

Question No. 1.—That the way to get rid of any habit is to cease to use it.

As every thing begins and ends in the *consciousness,* the way to stop using a thing is first to begin to stop thinking of it.

A *consciousness of economy* destroys, through disuse, one's power to create; it closes the channel to our creative power.

Question No. 2.—As the result of the practice of economy man has been developing a race *consciousness and thought habit* of limitation which has gradually separated him from the abundance of the supply of everything.

This *consciousness and thought habit* of *economy* has become so deep seated in many of the race that it extends even to their use of air with the result, it is now claimed by medical science, that 75 per cent of the children born are predisposed to the dread disease tuberculosis.

The human race must soon begin to learn the constructive use of everything and cease its *economizing* in the use of anything or its power to use things constructively will continue to grow less and less.

Question No. 3.—When we use them with the *consciousness,* the thought, the *feeling,* of being really able to get some good *use* out of them, rather than with the *consciousness,* thought or *feeling* of *economizing* or saving.

Question No. 4.—That it is the *consciousness,* the thought, the *feeling,* back of our act, not the act itself, which determines whether the effect on us is constructive or destructive, harmonious or inharmonious.

This is not only fundamental in the *Sears Philosophy,* but it is especially distinctive to the *Sears Philosophy* for it has never been taught elsewhere in the history of the world.

Question No. 5.—It feels poor. Every Nation suffers from business stagnation as the result of its *economy consciousness.*

The more it teaches and practises *economy* the greater becomes its reason for such practice and the more acute the necessity for it.

Question No. 6.—Buying was limited to the barest of necessities, and business everywhere came to such a sudden standstill the Government became frightened at the effect.

So great and sudden was the change the Government at once sent out an appeal for the people to spend some of their money and not completely stop the commercial life of the country.

Question No. 7.—The people did not respond so suddenly and so the effect was more gradual, but none the less the same as in 1917.

Factories of all kinds were closed down; thousands of men thrown out of employment; strikes indulged in; employers cutting down wages; business demoralized; stocks and bonds reached new low levels in price; and all this the outcome of man growing a *consciousness of economy* and so shutting himself off from the universal supply.

Question No. 8.—Most destructive, first, because the apparent necessity for *economy* implies limitation, a shortage in the supply, a necessity for lessening our use.

USE is the determining factor in universal law which governs man's relationship with supply, and when man cuts down his *use* of anything the universal law accepts his act as his standard and so gives him the lack which his non-use indicates he desires.

Destructive use, that is, use under the Law of Force, is also another sign to the universal law to curtail the supply for such use destroys.

Constructive use, that is, use under the

Law of Harmony, is the sign to the universal law to not only continue the supply, but to gradually increase it right along as fast as the user may be able to find additional constructive use for the increased supply.

It is never the thing we use it for which determines whether our use is constructive or destructive, but it is the *consciousness* with which we use it.

Question No. 9.—Man made. Because there is nothing in the Universe that practices *economy* except man.

As fast as the individual gets *big* enough to see this truth and then live it under the Law of Harmony does he cease to have need to practice *economy* in anything.

Question No. 10.—Abundance, profligacy, extravagance, everywhere. No limitations anywhere.

Take the matter of food as an illustration. Man is only limited in his supply by the amount of ground he prepares, plants and cultivates. In fact, he is not even limited to that for Nature provides an abundance of food in different sections of the world will he go where it is.

Question No. 11.—Through the *practice of economy,* that is, by depriving itself of many necessities and luxuries; denying itself many pleasures and enjoyments, and "saving" the money it would otherwise have expended for these things.

Question No. 12.—By *having a surplus* over and above that which it wanted to spend for necessities, luxuries, education, pleasure, entertainment, etc., and *knowing* that no matter how much money it expended "there was plenty more where it came from."

Question No. 13.—The extravagant *consciousness*, for it has a big enough vision to see the abundance of the supply, and when such a *consciousness* expresses the Law of Harmony its use of money and everything else is constructive.

Question No. 14.—Because that is the law such persons make for themselves, just as the other class make *economy* and its limited supply the law for them, and so the universal law works out in material form for us according to our model.

Question No. 15.—The fear habit. Because its *consciousness* always relates us with the inharmonious currents where the lack is to be found which causes us to believe the practice of *economy* is necessary.

Question No. 16.—Policy does not know the law and so is always looking for results and filled with doubt because they do not seem to come in just the way it expects.

Principle knows the universal law; knows it is unchangeable, immutable, irrevocable. Knowing this it also *knows* it is not necessary to keep looking for results. Results cannot help coming any more than the Sun can help shining.

The results may be obscured by darkness just as is the Sun sometimes, but the Sun still shines whether or not we see it, and the results of *principle* are there just as surely and in just the degree we have intelligently and harmoniously used the law.

Question No. 17.—No. Because it would mean death to the individual.

Blood is the physical vehicle which carries life to every part of the body and carries off the waste, the old and dead matter. To stop its flow would be to stop life in the body.

Money is to the commercial life of a Nation what blood is to the body, and the effect of the stoppage of the flow of money would be the same to its commerce as would the stoppage of the flow of blood be to the body, which is death.

Question No. 18.—Because the effect of its *economy* message was too plain to be misunderstood, and so the only thing to do was to get the people to begin spending their money again. Quick action was necessary or the life of the Nation would be imperiled to a far greater extent even than the war with Germany occasioned.

Question No. 19.—Destroying the *consciousness* of abundance.

Through decreased demand, and the non-use of our power to fill the demand, we gradually decrease our power and ability to supply even the lessened demand.

Creates a *consciousness* of separation from the abundance of the supply.

Gradually destroys our power and ability both to use and to create, as well as the incentive.

Question No. 20.—Because it is more subtle and far-reaching in its action; is not recognized nor understood as being either dangerous or destructive; it destroys incentive to use and create, and is everything a constructive and harmonious life does *not* want.

Answers to Questions

THE PSYCHOLOGY OF USE

OR

The Extravagance of Economy

Lesson Two

Question No. 1.—The subtle difference between *manipulating the universal Energy,* and that of only *manipulating the form,* whether such form be material or spiritual.

Question No. 2.—The manipulation of universal Energy by the *consciousness and thought habits.*

This means we first, knowingly, create what we want in our thought world, recognize our oneness with it now, and then see that only such thoughts as are harmonious in their *character* are allowed to come and persist with us.

Question No. 3.—The manipulation of the form.

This means attempting to influence the person or thing, whether such form be material or spiritual.

To attempt to persuade, coerce, bribe, force, make, compel, frighten, reward, punish, praise, or in any way control the action of either God or man in getting them to do that which we want done.

The motive back of our want, as well as the question of whether the external action is "good or bad," is immaterial.

The Author is aware this is the rankest kind of heresy to all our former teachings of science, philosophy and religion, but it is the greatest truth of them all, and he who really *wants* to prove its truth for himself can do so.

Question No. 4.—The *methods* used. *Methods* are the forms, ceremonies, rules, regulations, systems, technique, mode of procedure, man uses in doing things; in expressing the universal Energy.

Each sect, cult, class, political, social, business, economical and other division of society, claim their *method* is *the* only one which is right, and their *method* should therefore be used as a matter of *policy* without regard to any *principles* or universal laws it might violate.

The claim is further made that their *method* being *the* only one which is right it cannot therefore violate any principles, but is and must be infallible.

Question No. 5.—The *consciousness*

and thought habit with which the *method is used.*

No matter what *method* one may use, unless the *consciousness and thought habit,* the *feeling,* back of its use is harmonious and constructive, the effect on the user cannot be harmonious and constructive even though the user be highly successful otherwise, as gauged by the usual standards of man.

When the *consciousness and thought habit* is harmonious one can use any *method* he desires with success and the effect on him can only be constructive and harmonious.

Question No. 6.—No. One can only have a *consciousness* of lack and his inability to relate with the universal abundance of supply or he would not have the desire to save for the sake of saving. He would *know* there was no need of saving; that there was an abundance of everything; that he had a consciousness which was so harmonious and constructive it would never separate him from the abundance of the **supply**.

The *character* of a *consciousness* which finds it necessary to save gradually shuts one away from relating with abundance and so makes saving a necessity to such persons as long as they continue to grow that kind of a *consciousness.*

While the universal law they are using is unchangeable, immutable, irrevocable, their use of it is changeable and they can "about face" in their use of the law and begin to create a *consciousness and thought habit* which will relate them with the abundance instead of requiring them to continue the practice of *economy* and saving.

Question No. 7.—Because it has always spent its income lavishly, prodigally, extravagantly.

The Government of the United States has been controlled by politicians who recognized the only way they could retain their political power was by taking care of their henchmen, and this could only be done by providing for them at the expense of the Government.

The result could only be what it has been; a most lavish expenditure of Government income, and a constantly increasing income for the Government.

When we understand that the Government expended almost as much money in the two years following the declaration of war against Germany that it had expended in its entire history of over one hundred and forty years previous, we begin to have some idea of the prodigally *extravagant consciousness* which has been grown, especially by "the power behind the throne," that is, by the "invisible government" which is back of officialdom.

We also cease to wonder that there are those whose incomes amount to over twenty millions of dollars a year.

Had all this been done with a harmonious *consciousness and thought habit* back of it there could never be any inharmonious effect or reaction in the future, but as it has not, the inharmonious reaction will come in due time.

Question No. 8.—The *consciousness,* the thought habit, the *feeling,* with which it is spent and with which we review our action.

When we spend money with the *consciousness* and *feeling* of an abundance and our harmonious oneness with it; *knowing* we will relate with a constantly increasing supply under the Law of Harmony, we always will relate with it for that is law, universal law, unchangeable, immutable, irrevocable.

But when we allow fear, worry, anxiety, unrest, or inharmony of any kind to enter and remain in our thought world, the vibrations of such thoughts take us away from the universal currents of harmony, wherein is found the abundance of the supply of everything, and relates us with the universal currents of inharmony in which lack and limited supply are to be found and which makes the practice of *economy* necessary as long as we remain related to such currents.

Question No. 9.—Constructive. Its presence indicates the abundance of the supply and our oneness with it, otherwise there would not have been the surplus. We have an image, a vision, of opulence and abundance before us.

When we depend on the human mind for our image or vision we must have the materialized image before us; this strengthens our faith and belief, but when we learn the greater truth we create the image or vision with our *soul consciousness,* instead of our *human consciousness,* and see the universal abundance before us always, instead of being limited to the materialized supply.

Question No. 10.—Destructive. Such saving is the effect of denying one's self the things he wants and which would have made him happier, better, more harmonious and constructive; given him a bigger and broader vision of life; enabled him to feel his man-hood, which is only another name for one's God-self.

These things he felt he could not have and at the same time "save" that which he thought necessary to his future existence.

Such a *feeling,* or state of *consciousness,* can only result in growing a still greater *consciousness and thought habit* of lack which will separate one still more from the harmonious currents in which the universal abundance of the supply is to be found.

Question No. 11.—It gave them an objective image and vision of the materialized abundance of supply such as many of them had never dreamed of before.

It increased their range of vision and made bigger men and women out of them by reason thereof.

It is impossible for one to witness anything done on an immense scale without growing bigger in his own *consciousness*. Any other effect would be a violation of universal law.

The extent of such growth varies with each individual, but the least impressionable is affected to some extent.

Question No. 12.—Because of their *consciousness and thought habit* of inharmony.

We can obtain what we desire under either one of the two expressions of the law, force or harmonious attraction.

When we obtain it under the Law of Force our hold on it is precarious and continues only as long as we are able to exert a force which is stronger and greater than any we contact.

As the large majority cannot use force to the extent of the small minority, the prosperity of the masses, the people, cannot continue interrupted as long as it is created by them under the Law of Force.

Question No. 13.—The Law of Force. Because the reaction of the Law of Force upon its user is always disastrous and destructive.

The effect may come at once or in the ages yet to come, but it always comes for law is universal, immutable, unchangeable, irrevocable. That is why we know that its inharmonious use will always bring its reaction of inharmony to the user.

Our salvation lies in *changing our use* of universal law and so lifting us out of the inharmonious currents in which we have set all our inharmonious causes in motion, and in which we only can and do reap their inharmonious effects.

Question No. 14.—The universal law turns him back into the *character* of environment which accords with his development, his *consciousness.*

"A fountain can rise no higher than its source," and a life cannot remain long above or below the level of its own *consciousness.*

The methods and instruments used by the universal law for the above purpose are varied and numerous. Strikes, lockouts, loss of position, sickness, injury, theft, murder, love, hate, are only a few of the ways it is done or methods used.

Question No. 15.—The universal law under which we obtain it.

When we have used the Law of Force in obtaining a thing we are related with the universal currents of inharmony, and our use of things while remaining in these currents can only be inharmonious and destructive.

When we have used the Law of Harmony in obtaining a thing our *consciousness* relates us with the universal currents of harmony and our use of things while remaining related with these currents can only be harmonious and constructive.

Question No. 16.—Because universal law is unchangeable, immutable, irrevocable.

It is, therefore, impossible for man to relate with any person, thing, condition, or effect except as the result of the causes he himself has set in motion somewhere and sometime prior thereto.

We know this is true when we view life as a whole, a complete circle or cycle, instead of only the part of the circle which one human existence covers.

Any other solution of the question would make this a world of accident, chance, chaos; the plaything of some personal power which could work all kinds of injustices without any responsibility.

This would make such solution inequitable and unjust to the greatest degree, whereas one cannot find the slightest inequity or injustice in the solution offered by the *Sears-Philosophy*.

Question No. 17.—Because it is necessary for them to have a parentage and environment where the greatest freedom of thought and action may be had, and where there is the greatest opportunity for the growth and unfoldment of the soul along harmonious lines which the bigness of the country and the immensity of its wealth offers.

Question No. 18.—Because they had the thought, the *feeling*, the *consciousness*, of there always being "plenty more."

This *consciousness* was the connecting link and established the relationship between them and the universal abundance of supply by which the more they, as a Nation, used of the supply the more they had to use.

Question No. 19.—No. The entire history of the United States from the Declaration of Independence, more than one hundred and forty years ago, down to the present time, demonstrates *the extravagance of economy* and the truth of the universal law of constructive and harmonious *use* which these Lessons teach.

Question No. 20.—Grow and develop a *consciousness and thought habit* of harmony and our oneness with the universal abundance of the supply.

Because it is the *consciousness and thought habit* back of our expression, back of our use of Energy, which determines its effect on us.

When we express extravagance with an inharmonious *consciousness and thought habit,* the effect on us can only be destructive and disastrous.

But when we express extravagance with a harmonious *consciousness and thought habit* then the effect on us will always be constructive and cause us to continue relating with a constantly increasing supply.

Answers to Questions

THE PSYCHOLOGY OF USE

OR

The Extravagance of Economy

Lesson Three

Question No. 1.—That thought includes something more than man's mental or intellectual power, and is used by all forms, on all planes of consciousness.

Question No. 2.—Nature never *economizes* anywhere, but is most lavish in her expenditures of everything.

The great depths of space which reach out between worlds; the vast mountain ranges, the broad prairies, the great deserts, the forests; everything everywhere tells the story of Nature's prodigality and extravagance.

Nature knows the universal law of the abundance of everything, and that as long as the supply is used harmoniously it will continue to replenish itself automatically, that is, the replenishing is self-acting because of the universal law used.

Some persons have this *consciousness* of their oneness with the abundance of the supply so deeply stamped upon some of the cells of their body that they grow a third set of teeth.

Those who do not do this are those who either do not need the third set, or who have created such a *consciousness* of separation they think they can't grow another set and so do not.

Nature does not deny them a sufficient supply of "raw material" with which to grow the third set of teeth, but such persons fail to use it for that purpose because of the *character* and kind of *consciousness* they have grown.

Question No. 3.—Because his *consciousness and thought habit* are too inharmonious and his *consciousness* or sense of separation from abundance too great, to permit him to relate with the supply.

This is why the miser starves to death although there is an abundance of food all around him and he has plenty of money with which to purchase it.

His *economy consciousness* has created such a perfect and complete *consciousness* or sense of separation that it will not allow him to spend his money for the food necessary to keep his body alive, and so it dies.

In the death of his body the miser performs the last act necessary to complete the materialized effect of his *consciousness* of separation from abundance, for he separates himself from the only thing he had left—his money.

Question No. 4.—He first creates a *consciousness* of his separation from that particular thing in which he is *economizing*.

When he persists in the practice of *economy,* this *consciousness* of separation gradually grows and increases until in time he unknowingly applies it to all things.

This is why we have people who lack everything one might desire, health, money, friends, love, home. They have separated themselves so completely from everything in their *consciousness* that they have become the outcasts of the world.

However, they are only reaping the harvest of the seed they have ignorantly and unconsciously sown by their thoughts in the past.

Question No. 5.—We ultimately lose our ability to use it. Continued failure or refusal to use our faculties or power can only result in our growing a *consciousness* which does not know how to use them.

Since "eating of the tree of knowledge of good and evil and becoming wise as gods," man has failed to use the discriminating power of his will and so permit only thoughts of a constructive and harmonious *character* to enter and remain in his human mind.

The result is his will-power has lost the power to exclude the inharmonious thoughts because of man's non-use of such power, or his use of it under the Law of Force.

Thinking inharmonious thoughts; putting the destructive interpretation on what others say, think, or do, has become "natural" to man, although it should and would be the most *unnatural and impossible* thing had he used his will-power rightly in the past.

Question No. 6.—Yes. While it is much more difficult to awaken, revive and revitalize a faculty deadened from disuse or injured and impaired from destructive use, yet it can be done but it requires continued, persistent, patient work on our part.

Question No. 7.—By *ceasing to use them;* allowing them to atrophy from disuse.

This is a most wonderful and yet

simple statement of fact which is true although entirely new.

When we *cease to use* anything it begins to *cease to exist for us.*

We begin to cease relating with conditions which call forth its use.

Its hold on us grows less and less secure until finally it ceases altogether.

We know it no more for we do not relate with the currents in which need for its use is to be found.

Question No. 8.—We unconsciously and unknowingly create a *consciousness* of separation which applies only to money at first, but as it is persisted in this *consciousness* of separation is gradually extended to apply to health, love, friends, and other things.

So all-absorbing has this *consciousness* of separation become in many persons that it even separates them from air and causes them to be born in a human body and environment which predisposes them to tuberculosis. This is why that dread disease has made such rapid strides in the last half century.

Question No. 9.—Because the soul carries its *consciousness* of separation with it from incarnation to incarnation, just as the human mind carries its *consciousness* with it from day to day.

This causes it to continue to be born in a body and environment of constantly increasing poverty and lack until it ceases to create the *consciousness* of separation which is the outgrowth of the practice of *economy* and other inharmonious thought habits.

Question No. 10.—Dualistic. Because

he is both material and spiritual; human and divine.

This kind of a combination is necessary in order that the coarser and more undeveloped human side may be refined and developed through close contact with the finer or divine expression.

Also that through such close contact the divine man might increase his knowledge, wisdom and understanding and so become a still better instrument through which Energy, Life, God, might express.

Question No. 11.—Human man expresses the physical and mental; divine man, the soul and spiritual.

Through the close contact and association of human and divine man, the latter obtains a vehicle through which it can express its larger vision and deeper understanding to the unfolding human man's *consciousness* and so give the latter a greater ideal and a bigger standard from which to work in his growth and unfoldment.

It is in this way that man has obtained the knowledge, wisdom and understanding which has made possible the wonderful civilization of the present century.

Human man in turn is able to express through divine man's faculties, the messages and instructions he wishes to give to the intelligence expressing in the lesser forms he contacts, the atoms of his body and environment.

This is how all so-called "miracles" are performed.

Question No. 12.—He ultimately became sated, lazy, indolent, shiftless, without ambition or desire. Being one with all life in his *consciousness,* he had every desire satisfied as soon as it was formulated.

This was why, when he created the desire to "become wise as gods and know good from evil," such desire was at once satisfied.

The living in a *consciousness* which recognized evil or inharmony soon created a *consciousness* or *feeling* which separated him from good or harmony, and so brought him into only the kind of relationships, such as sickness, disease, anger, hate, poverty and lack, as made for still greater inharmony.

Question No. 13.—In human man's *consciousness and thought habit* first, and then in his material world.

The human and astral bodies of man remain connected on the astral plane as long as the human body continues to "live." "Death" never occurs until the separation of the two bodies takes place on the astral plane.

Question No. 14.—Thought. This is not simply mental power or mental force as we have been taught to believe in the past.

It is something entirely different from that. It is a universal power which all form uses, whether animate or inanimate, visible or invisible, material or spiritual.

..*Question No. 15.*—It is the effect of the *use* of this universal power, thought, by the mental or intellectual faculty of the human mind.

Question No. 16.—It is the effect of the *use* of this same universal power, thought, by the soul mind.

The soul mind, being a finer vehicle through which to use thought than is the human mind, its use of this universal power, thought, is much stronger, more powerful, far-reaching and subtle than is its use by the human mind.

Things which are impossible or very difficult of accomplishment by the human mind's use of thought, become easy of accomplishment when thought is used by the soul mind.

Question No. 17.—The limited currents of the material world in which only the limited expression of things is to be found.

It is in these limited and inharmonious currents that man relates with sickness, disease, poverty and lack of all kinds, and where he finds the "can'ts" and "impossibles" of his everyday life.

Everything is either difficult or impossible of accomplishment in these currents and man has to fight and *economize* as long as he remains related with them in his *consciousness*.

Question No. 18.—The unlimited universal currents.

This is where man relates with health, wealth, love, happiness, joy, and the abundance of everything he desires.

Nothing is difficult of accomplishment while he is related with these currents, for he recognizes (consciously or unconsciously) his oneness with everything he desires under the Law of Harmony.

There are no "if's, can'ts, nor impossibles" in his vocabulary as long as he remains related with these currents in his *consciousness*.

Question No. 19.—Because he only contacts and relates with the materialized supply—never with the unlimited supply of "raw material" from which the materialized supply is made.

Human man's *consciousness* of the abundance of the universal substance, the "raw material," from which everything is made, is somewhat analogous to the *consciousness* and knowledge of a layman entering a manufacturing establishment about which he knows nothing.

The layman, seeing only the manufactured product, and knowing nothing of the source from which the "raw materials" are obtained, nor the abundance of the supply, thinks only of the limited manufactured product and so sees and thinks of the supply as being small and limited.

And it is small and limited to him for his very thought attitude makes it so, and only relates him with the limited portion of the supply.

Divine man is like the manager of the factory, in that he knows all about the abundance of the supply of "raw materials" from which the manufactured product is made, their source and how to relate with them.

He knows that the more he *uses* of the "raw materials" in the manufacture of his product the more of the "raw materials" will there be for him to use.

The supply of the "raw materials" is governed by his *use* of them. This supply increases the more he uses them, and decreases when he begins to "economize" in their use.

Divine man *knows* the abundance of "raw material," that is, the universal substance from which all things are made, is inexhaustible, and that just as man increases the muscles of his body through their harmonious and constructive use, so does he increase the amount of the universal substance with which he relates and differentiates into money, health, love, and whatever else he may desire, the more he uses it harmoniously and constructively.

Divine man *knows* that in this way does he really "eat his cake and have it too."

Question No. 20.—It enlarges his conception of life; gives him a bigger vision and a deeper understanding; makes of him a better vehicle through which life may express; enables him to encompass the entire circle of life instead of only the small portion covered by the existence of one human body.

It enables him to lift his human self

only relates him with the limited portion of the supply.

Divine man is like the manager of the factory, in that he knows all about the abundance of the supply of "raw materials" from which the manufactured product is made, their source and how to relate with them.

He knows that the more he *uses* of the "raw materials" in the manufacture of his product the more of the "raw materials" will there be for him to use.

The supply of the "raw materials" is governed by his *use* of them. This supply increases the more he uses them, and decreases when he begins to "economize" in their use.

Divine man *knows* the abundance of "raw material," that is, the universal substance from which all things are made, is inexhaustible, and that just as man increases the muscles of his body through their harmonious and constructive use, so does he increase the amount of the universal substance with which he relates and differentiates into money, health, love, and whatever else he may desire, the more he uses it harmoniously and constructively.

Divine man *knows* that in this way does he really "eat his cake and have it too."

Question No. 20.—It enlarges his conception of life; gives him a bigger vision and a deeper understanding; makes of him a better vehicle through which life may express; enables him to encompass the entire circle of life instead of only the small portion covered by the existence of one human body.

It enables him to lift his human self

out of the inharmonious and limited currents of the material plane of sickness, disease, poverty and lack, and relate him with the unlimited currents in which is found the abundance of everything he desires and which goes to make life here both livable and lovable.

This price list in force on and after March 1st, 1920
subject to change without notice

Sears Philosophy
makes life livable and lovable
"The Books Without an If"
teach how

CENTRE PUBLISHING CO,
108 & 110 W. 34th St., New York.

Please send me the following books by F. W. Sears, M.P., for which I enclose $....................in payment.

Sears Philosophy—What it Teaches............	$ .35
Concentration—Its Mentology and Psychology, Paper,	50
" " " " " Cloth	75
How to Attract Success...........Cloth...........	2.00
Sears Psychology Lessons, Vol I, "	1.50
" " " " II, "	1.50
" Philosophy " " III., "	1.50
How to Give Treatments............................	1.50
How to Conquer Fear, Library Edition, Cloth.........	1 00
" " " " Pocket " "	.75
" " " " " " " Paper.........	50
Everyday Experiences..................Cloth.........	.75
The Mysteries of Sleep................Paper........	.35
Was Jesus God or Man? .... "	35
The Three Monkeys................... "	.35
The Unlimited Supply................ "	.35
Am I to Blame?...................... "	.35
Who Made God?...................... "	35
What Is Truth?...................... "	.35
The Angel Back of Us............... "	35

Any three 35c. books for $1.00

Correspondence Course of 12 Lessons on ⎫ Price and terms
   Concentration and Will Power....... ⎬ . of payment
Correspondence Course of 30 Lessons on ⎭   given on
   The Psychology of Abundance....... application
Correspondence Course of 3 Lessons on
   The Psychology of Use, or
   The Extravagance of Economy.................10 00

Name..

No...*Street*

........................*City*.....................*State*

www.ingramcontent.com/pod-product-compliance
Ingram Content Group UK Ltd.
Pitfield, Milton Keynes, MK11 3LW, UK
UKHW020707090725
6803UKWH00012B/133